Always COLORADO

by Jon Sheppard

Designed by:
Daryl Stevens @ www.studio202.com
350 Third Avenue #317, New York, NY 10010. 212 741 1610.

If there are errors in names, places, or things the author apologizes.
P.O. Box 18101, Avon. CO. 81620
jonshepp@vail.net
JonSheppardPhotography.com

9 8 7 6 5 4 3 2 1

Library of Congress Catalog Card Number 98-96794

Sheppard, J. 1942

Always Colorado

Photography

1. Non-fiction - Authorship, 1. Title II.
Title: Always Colorado.

0-9658009-1-1

Printed and bound in Korea

Opposite: Alpine Daisy

May the God of Heaven and the world above
Bring you peace and happiness filled with love
Something to have and someone to hold
Always to share and never grow old.

To Ken & Ruth Sheppard
Sixty years of togetherness

Fairy Trumpet

Opposite: San Juan Mountains

4

One day as I was climbing high in the Sawatch Mountains, the sun was bright and warm.
Clouds bellowed a brilliant white against a sky of blue. This is Colorado.

Opposite: Sunset above timberline.

Preface

My first book, *Someday in a Place Out West,* was an exhilarating experience. I have been richly rewarded by all the letters, phone calls, and face to face comments from many of you who have a copy. For those who don't have the book, please look for it. Rest assured, you will be deeply blessed. I would also like to thank Dorothy Buel, Bruce Chatterton and Cathy Hebert, special friends who helped me edit this book and *Someday in a Place Out West.*

I am glad to share these images of Colorado with you. They were shot over an extended period of time, encompassing all the changing seasons. It has been fun traveling, meeting people, and photographing throughout the state. Let your hearts and minds drift and travel into another adventure in this beautiful country called Colorado. When you are out on the great eastern prairies, driving over the next hill, or climbing up in the high country, excitement awaits you. Whenever you camp by a bubbling mountain stream, let the sound of the rolling waters relax your mind. Listen to the wind blowing through the aspen trees. Watch the sky as it turns into a golden melting pot of pink, red, and purple. And, as the day slowly turns into night, the stars will fall right down to your finger tips.

When the snow falls in the high country get ready to snowmobile, snowshoe, back country ski, or rip downhill at one of Colorado's wonderful ski resorts. Visit where people seldom travel and marvel at the smooth, poetic lines etched in the snow by the sun and wind. As spring slowly surfaces, first from the lowlands and then into the higher elevations, watch as the flowers and trees sprout their new color of life. Enjoy the feel of waving grasses in a sea of green as a gentle breeze caresses your face. Participate in the joy of summer. Watch the tumbling rivers as the snow melts from distant peaks. Raft the challenging whitewater or find a quiet pond where you can sit and meditate, alone or with a friend. Pack a picnic lunch. Fish the back country streams or hike a high country meadow. If you are full of adventure climb a 14,000 foot mountain. As autumn rounds the corner drive along one of the many scenic byways and marvel at the fall colors. Walk a trail covered with leaves. Listen to the bugling of the elk. Watch the skyward processions of geese and other birds as they migrate south. Share the wonders with someone special. It's beautiful. It's yours for the asking, and it's . . . *Always Colorado.*

Grey Jay

Ptarmigan

Previous page: The Flattops Wilderness looking southeast to the New York Mountains.

Opposite: Bristlecone Pine

Mr. Owl

Fall

When the shimmering leaves fall gently to the ground you know that the autumn season has come, and winter is right down the road, or over the mountain top. In fact, there is already a dusting of white way above timberline. At night the temperature slips into the lower 30's. During the day the fall sun is at its special brilliance, warming up into the 60's and 70's. For now it's a beautiful landscape of yellows, reds, browns, and darker green. The powder white clouds are billowing up into an azure blue sky, and there is a cool but gentle breeze flowing across the valley. The elk and deer are in the fall rutting season. Hunters are trying for their trophy and a winters supply of food for their families. Many migrating birds are heading south for warmer winter feeding grounds. The butterflies and humming birds have long since made their way to Mexico.

Friends and families are out in the wilderness camping and enjoying day hikes. Happy people are horseback riding around a shimmering wilderness lake, or on a multi-day pack trip into the high country. ATV's are humming the old back roads while other outdoorsmen are fishing a cold mountain stream for that big, elusive fat trout. Some people are exploring long-abandoned mining towns that are now ghost towns. Climbers are going for their next 14,000 foot mountain. There is a couple relaxing in the warm rays of the afternoon sun on the deck of their log cabin home. They are enjoying, not only the panoramic vista in front of them, but time together. At night around the campfire, friends sit and enjoy their cups of hot chocolate as the stars twinkle in the quiet blackness which surrounds them. And some of us are out grabbing a shot of the last fall colors before all the leaves are gone and the sun dips behind the mountains to the west.

Opposite: Mt. Sneffels, San Juan Mountains

14

Cattails stand in the afternoon light.

Opposite: Red berries hang above the clear waters of the Crystal River.

I hiked a trail covered in freshly fallen leaves. There had been an overnight freeze and now the sun had melted the frost into water droplets on this aspen leaf. I have found such beauty in my travels.

Opposite: Courthouse Mountain near Owl Creek Pass.

I love big animals and I especially love big cats. This is Shayla. She lives outside of Telluride at the Rocky Mountain Ark Wildlife Rehabilitation Center. Her older sister, Ruby, was in my last book. Lissa Margetts has kept her animal shelter and rehab program going quite well. Whenever I am in the area, I always try to go by and visit all of her animals, my favorites being the BIG cats.

Opposite: The Maroon Bells Snowmass Wilderness area is one of the ten most photographed scenes in America. So here is my version. Photographed in October, the fall colors were still there. An overnight snowstorm left a white cover on the mountains. With a slight chill in the air, the sky was a deep Colorado blue. Enjoy it as I did.

Following page: Willows School in the wet mountain valley. Horn Peak is in the background.

The bottles in the window of this cabin reflect the late afternoon light.
The town is Tincup and is filled with homes and their stories of the past.

Old towns, ghost towns, and restored towns dot the valleys. You will enjoy "South Park City" in Fairplay.

Without a good rope and tack gear, the cowboy is out of business. They always take care of their equipment and their horses.

And the cowboy is still the heart of the West. Whether riding in a rodeo, checking a fence line,
or moving cattle from one place to another, he is the man.

I was traveling to Rocky Mountain National Park at sun rise one fall day and found a fog bank along the way. The trees and grass were covered in frost. What a way to start the day!

This is a special Timber wolf. Her name is Cheyenne and loves to be visited by women and children. As for we men, she keeps her distance. Mark Johnson is her human leader and spends his time working with her for various wildlife and conservation events. Cheyenne has her own press credentials and has been writing a weekly column in the *Mountain Messenger* out of Idaho Springs for three years. You can reach Cheyenne on the internet: visionswest_art.com.

Following page: 14,005 foot Mount Huron from Cottonwood Pass

Whether fishing, riding a bike, or just relaxing, people and friends are the center of life.

Opposite: Lands End Road, Grand Mesa

Following page: I had been shooting fall colors around Owl Creek Pass and was returning west, towards Ridgway, on a wide, gravel road. Off to my left I saw two riders in an open field. This was one shot that I did not want to miss. At about forty miles an hour I slammed on my brakes and slid fifty yards or more to a stop with dust and gravel flying everywhere. I hollered to the riders and met a wonderful couple from the Sawtooth Mountain Ranch. They were most gracious and let me photograph them as they were looking for some of their cattle in the afternoon light. Finished, we headed our own separate ways.

Falling water, enjoy it with a friend.

Come join me for an exciting fall train ride on the Tolec Cumberes Scenic Railroad. The train starts in Antonito, found at the southern end of the San Luis Valley. Winding it's way through the Rio Grande national Forest, it climbs to 10,022 foot Cumbres Pass. There they stop and refill the steam engine from the original water tank tower. From there the train drops about fourteen miles into the New Mexico town of Chama. The fall colors were fabulous the day that I was there. People on the train were taking pictures and waved as it chugged on to its rendezvous with Chama in the mid-afternoon sun.

Winter

Snow falls early in the high country. Above timberline, the on-coming season could be evident by the first of October. When the trees are bare, and the mountain streams have slowed to a quiet trickle, the winds of winter bring beautiful flakes of white to lay a gentle cover over the land. Squirrels and porcupines have stored up for the long days ahead. The bears are in their dens starting a snooze that will last until spring. Deer and elk are moving down to lower elevations finding food wherever they can.

As the snow falls deeper and the mountains are cloaked in white, there is a fascinating change in the land and the people. Young and retired alike find their way to the resorts for a season of winter fun. There is a hum of hyper-activity as the ski companies ready themselves for the coming season. The race is on to see which ski area will be the first to open. Skiers and snowboarders are in line, long before sunrise, to be the first. The expected usually occurs before Halloween. First one, then another. Soon all are wheeling the lifts and it's ski time in the Rockies!

Wonderful people from across the nation, and around the world, come for a week or two of winter fun. From beginners to experts, ski school or snowboarding classes, it's what we are all here to enjoy. The magnetic power of the snowcovered runs brings exhilaration and relaxation.

There is the hustle and bustle at the airports. The long shuttle ride brings you to your destination. Lodges, brimming with excitement and activity, are ready for your arrival. The ski shops, stores, and a tempting array of restaurants will keep you on the go. The white powder beckons you. Don't waste a minute. You may wish to feel the luxury of sleeping until 10 in the morning, or, be up at the crack of dawn to skim the slopes until sundown. The choice is yours.

Sliding and gliding down a long groomed run you carve a beautiful turn, and then another and another. Your favorite powder run is untracked. As you plow through knee deep powder all you can think of is the next perfect turn. There is an adrenalin rush that only those who experience it know. A euphoric joy overcomes you with a thrill you can only feel in your heart. You have forgotten all about work, those appointments you made for next week, or even dinner plans for the evening. At that moment, skiing or snowboarding is King! Share this perfect day with friends and family.

How about a dog sled ride? When the musher takes control and the dogs are off and running, it's rock and roll! Listen to them bark with excitement. Watch them as they charge through the snow. Enjoy the pristine forests as you travel through the wilderness. For those who want more excitement, let's go for a snowmobile ride up above timberline. On a clear day you can see snow white mountains stretch all across the wide horizon. Please bring your camera. A horseback riding trip during the day or a horse drawn sleigh in the evening light is full of fun and romance, especially if you're with that special person. A wonderful dinner afterwards will make the day complete.

For a slower pace, try snowshoeing in the back country or go cross country skiing with some fellow skiers. The soothing rush of an excited heart, is forever. Listen! The silence of the wilderness is golden.

Tomorrow will be a new day!

Fences do more than just stake a property line or keep the livestock from wandering off their own land. They tell of days and times of the past. Take note of how fences are put up. The materials that were used. What kind of wire is it? Did they get the wood from nearby forests or did they have to carry it in from other places? Once again the old fences have a story of their own. Listen to the wind "singing" through the barbed wire as it tells a tale of long ago.

These horses love to run in the snow, especially when I am sitting on their feed truck. My friends, Tom and Carol Rupert, have a ranch in the mountains near Snowmass. As for these big, beautiful animals, they are gentle riding critters and love to be fed and pampered.

For the first two weeks of February 1999, the world of alpine skiing flocked to Vail and Beaver Creek for the World Cup Championships ski races. In the history of the World Cup racing, this would be the third time the race was held in the United States. You had to be here to witness the totality of the event. About 1500 plus volunteers transported VIP's, checked tickets, served food, acted as hosts, and helped wherever needed.

The race course workers were on the course by 6AM on race days to groom the run to perfection. Support staff of every nature was there to meet the many needs of the spectators and racers. The crowds, the excitement, the tremendous speeds of the down hill and media from all over, made for a most unique world class event. Although only one racer brought home his gold medal, to me, all who raced were winners. I was ecstatic just to be here. The whole world was invited. It was billed as "The Last Great Race of the 20th Century." . . . And it was!

On our world record breaking, "Ski eighteen in one day," we were at Arapahoe Basin by 7AM. At that time we had already skied five ski areas. We also raised over $20,000 for the US Disabled Ski Team.

Carving perfect turns.

Opposite: Longs Peak. It's found in Rocky Mountain National Park and one heck of a very long, all day climb. You can see a part of the infamous Diamond as the storm clouds of winter are blowing in cold, dry snow. The hard core climb it in weather like this.

A storm moves in on Mount Evans.

Opposite: Roads will take you through green, fertile valleys, or among the high, snow capped peaks. You can cruise over the high country passes, and to places or times from long ago. It will softly touch your inner spirit with joy, peace, and relaxation.

It's amazing how these trees of long ago grew and grew and spiraled towards the sky.

Opposite: An afternoon summer thunderstorm brewing in the San Luis Valley.

Grand Mesa

Spring

The days are growing longer now. It's wonderful to see the sun rising earlier in the mornings and lingering on into the evening hours. March is our biggest snow fall month, with warm weather not far behind. When we are lucky, the weather gives us bonus days allowing some ski areas to stay open into June and July. Skiing in shorts and Tee shirts is a wonderful spring time rush. We've come to another change in seasons and everyone is feeling the rebirth of nature.

People are planning their next adventure. So many choices . . . hikes into the back country or snow hikes into the high country. The mountain creeks and streams are slowly bubbling and rippling with new life. The rush of the snowmelt is yet to come. River running programs are starting to stir again.

In the valleys, the snow is melting away, the grass is turning green, and buds begin to appear on the trees. In a short time flowers will be popping up everywhere. Joggers and walkers are in the warm sunshine. Moms and dads are taking their children to nearby parks. The birds have started to return to build their nests and start their families. Animals are having their young. Butterflies and humming birds are returning from Mexico. It's a time to reflect on the wonderful memories of skiing and look forward to the coming of summer.

Life is fresh, new, and exciting.

Tiger Lilly

The summer wild flowers in the fading evening light are found in a high mountain meadow.
A wonderful way to end the day.

Hot air ballooning can be found throughout the mountain towns. On this early summer morning they were lifting off from Steamboat Springs. When you drift high above the surrounding countryside, and it's as quiet as a sleeping baby, you will find yourself breathing new life into your heart.

Opposite: Sit and enjoy the beauty of Colorado.

The Great Sand Dunes

The cabins that were built so very long ago are slowly fading away through time, fire, weather, and the progress of man. Explore them, photograph them, keep them in your heart. For soon they will be no more.

Goats Beard in seed

In beautiful and historic Leadville stands the classic Delaware Hotel. Stop in and visit as I did on a full moon night

Opposite: The World Cup party in Beaver Creek.

Summer

The days are warm and sunny now. Flowers are colorful and abundant. People are on the go. Rivers and streams are full to overflowing with the winter's snowmelt. The high country is opening up for all to visit. Try Trail Ridge Road in Rocky Mountain National Park, Independence Pass, or other scenic byways. As the roads clear, snow remains on the mountain sides. Visit the alpine areas and view the beautiful array of wild flowers. Your mind and heart will skip with excitement.

Watch for marmot, deer, elk, and other mountain critters feeding from sun up to sun down. Lakes are full to the brim and waiting for boaters, fishing folks, or those who would view their beauty. Excellent camping areas are to be found throughout the state.

After an isolated afternoon thunderstorm, make a wish on the pastel arches of a rainbow that appears as if by magic. Fish that quiet pond or cool mountain stream. Whitewater rafting brings an incomparable thrill to first timers or experienced rafters. Whether one is on a mellow float trip on the upper Colorado or crashing into Class IV or V rapids, the trip can be both serene and breathtaking. We have many visitors and locals kayaking, canoeing, or rafting on short sections of a river or they may be taking day trips into a distant canyon. The choice is yours.

How about a visit to a ghost town or historic mining town? The buildings stand as a testament of another era and time in America. Some of the locals have been here for many generations. The stories they can relate could take you back in time. Horse pack trips into the wilderness areas will conjure up visions of the western frontier of yesteryear. Catch any of the shows and pageants which come to life in the "old west" towns. The "shoot-em ups" always draw a crowd.

Entertain yourselves by visiting the outstanding arts and crafts festivals, summer concerts, and rodeos. The largest Fourth of July fireworks show in the state is found in Avon. You will be surrounded with music, fun and happy people from all over. Oh yes! Don't forget the summer rodeos. You will find them everywhere.

From the Great Sand Dunes in the south central area, to the deeply carved canyons of the Western Slope, Colorado can fulfill your wish for the exciting, the magnificent, the beautiful.

With this everchanging panorama of life, the only element lacking is finding the time to photograph all the scenes I want to capture with my camera's lens. And I live here!

Opposite: Grand Mesa

Following Page: Colorado Sunflowers

Columbine, Colorado's state flower.

Opposite: Blanca Peak massive in the San Luis Valley.

Water. Sometimes it's frozen, sometimes it's a falling frozen flake. Sometimes it's a smooth, poetic mirror reflecting a beautiful sunrise. Sometimes it's a silky, velvety flow over ledges and rocks whispering soothing music on a quiet mountain stream. Enjoy it with a special friend.

The surf is up and all are there, sharing a wonderful glass wave on the Colorado River. As I listened closely you could hear them discussing the topic of the day. Who has the car keys? Did you remember to lock the car? Who brought lunch? And, the men's room is on down stream!

Opposite: Scott Young on a wet adventure.

Following Page: A deep velvet of green and water.

Reflections happen when you may least expect them. Search for them and watch for them. They are very special.

Paint Brush

Violet

Opposite: The San Juan Mountains in the fall.

I have always had a fascination for flowers. They are beautiful and found everywhere. The columbine is found throughout the high country. This group was photographed on the Flat Tops Wilderness.

Opposite: Enyoy a hike to Shrine Pass

Opposite: "I met her at the sand dunes on a windy summer day."

Yarrow with an albino spider.

Mallow

Opposite: Looking North at Blue Lake high above Independence Pass.

Glenwood Hot Springs Pool on a clear fall afternoon.

The autumn frost has arrived.

Opposite: Cottonwood Pass

Windows and local murals

St. Elmo

The buildings still stand in St. Elmo. In fact, the semi-ghost town is on the National Record of Historical Places. St. Elmo nestles in between Mt. Princeton and Mt. Antero, and you will find it about thirteen miles up a side canyon from the Arkansas River Valley. Along the way you will pass over tempting Mt. Princeton Hot Springs. You will find many camping spots, and a few beaver ponds that dot the roadside. People live in St. Elmo all year long, but most of the folks are there only in the summer. Wander casually along the main street and visit some of the stores. Owners will tell you about the history of the area. Please take the time and feed the always hungry chipmunks while you are there.

Opposite: Fireweed and a fresh mountain stream.

Following page: Alpine Daisy Flat Tops wilderness area.

And another chapter has closed but not forgotten. With joy, peace, and love I have shared with you this beautiful country, Colorado. I thank God for letting me travel, photograph, and write my stories. You have enjoyed thrilling trips over the highways, the byways, and up on the snow filled mountaintops. Please join me and all my friends in my next adventure, *Cowboys, Cowgirls and Wide Open Spaces.*